VOCABULARY
SUCCESS STAGE II

IVY LEAGUE

Icon English Ivy League Vocabulary Success Stage II

Copyright © 2019 by Icon English Institute

No part of this publication may be reproduced, distributed, or transmitted in any form or by any means, including photocopying, recording, or other electronic or mechanical methods, without the prior written permission of the author, except in the case of brief quotations embodied in critical reviews and certai other non-commercial uses permitted by copyright law.

Icon English
www.iconenglish.com

TABLE OF CONTENTS

Stage Two A

- Lesson One 10
- Lesson Two 12
- Lesson Three 14
- Lesson Four 16
- Lesson Five 18
- Lesson Six 20
- Lesson Seven 22
- Lesson Eight 24
- Lesson Nine 26
- Lesson Ten 28
- Lesson Eleven 30
- Lesson Twelve 32
- Lesson Thirteen 34
- Lesson Fourteen 36
- Lesson Fifteen 38
- Lesson Sixteen 40
- Lesson Seventeen 42
- Lesson Eighteen 44
- Lesson Nineteen 46
- Lesson Twenty 48
- Lesson Twenty one 50
- Lesson Twenty two 52
- Lesson Twenty three 54
- Lesson Twenty four 56
- Lesson Twenty five 57
- Lesson Twenty six 60
- Lesson Twenty seven 62
- Lesson Twenty eight 64
- Lesson Twenty nine 66
- Lesson Thirty 68

TABLE OF CONTENTS

Stage Two B

- Lesson One 72
- Lesson Two 74
- Lesson Three 76
- Lesson Four 78
- Lesson Five 80
- Lesson Six 82
- Lesson Seven 84
- Lesson Eight 86
- Lesson Nine 88
- Lesson Ten 90
- Lesson Eleven 92
- Lesson Twelve 94
- Lesson Thirteen 96
- Lesson Fourteen 98
- Lesson Fifteen 100
- Lesson Sixteen 102
- Lesson Seventeen 104
- Lesson Eighteen 106
- Lesson Nineteen 108
- Lesson Twenty 110
- Lesson Twenty one 112
- Lesson Twenty two 114
- Lesson Twenty three 116
- Lesson Twenty four 118
- Lesson Twenty five 120
- Lesson Twenty six 122
- Lesson Twenty seven 124
- Lesson Twenty eight 126
- Lesson Twenty nine 128
- Lesson Thirty 130

INTRODUCTION

Icon English Ivy League Vocabulary Success is a series of books, each of which is intended for you to use when learning English. What's great about our books is that they can be used either with a teacher in a classroom setting or independently in your own time.

Vocabulary is one of the most vital aspects of learning a language. Without a rich vocabulary, how do you express the things you want to say? Furthermore, many students will find that having a vast lexicon can be a huge help when taking exams or writing essays for school. And, though some words may not be used in everyday conversations, less common words are still important to learn for certain assignments or standardized tests. Language is varied and complex. Your vocabulary should be that way too.

To keep things simple, each lesson is comprised of ten words. Their meanings, forms and parts of speech need your full attention so that you can learn how to determine which word in what form works best in which fill-in-the-blank sentence. After the sentences, you will read a passage. These passages contain the same ten words from your vocabulary lesson. Reading these words in a narrative context will help you understand how these words are used, and how you can apply them yourself.

WHO IS THIS SERIES AIMED AT?

STAGE ZERO:
BASIC

Stage Zero begins with a "dead word" and a word list. We call words like happy, tired, or pretty "dead" because they are so overused that their meanings fall flat. Included beneath each "dead word" are other, more complicated words with similar meanings. Stage Zero will help you precisely express what you're trying to say without resorting to stale language. Each word list is sorted into categories so that you can really concentrate your language and distinguish yourself for excellent diction whenever you speak or write in English.

STAGE I:
INTERMEDIATE

After completing Stage Zero, you will have absorbed many intriguing new words. However, Stage I is different. These lessons are aimed at high school students who want to improve their writing skills. Many high school assignments require students to analyze complicated works of literature, but how can you complete those difficult assignments if you can't comprehend the words being used? Stage I will help you discover new, complicated words that you will come across in your classes. Boost your essay marks by completing Stage I!

STAGE II:
ADVANCED

Stage II covers some of the complex words in the English language. Much like Stage I, Stage II will provide you with a word list (plus their part of speech and meaning), fill-in-the-blank sentences, and a short passage. The words in Stage II were chosen by combing through SAT tests from the past few years and picking out the most common words used. However, even if you don't plan on taking the SAT's or ACT's, Stage II is still a vital part of helping you become a fluent speaker and writer of English! Take your skills to the next level and conquer Stage II!

STAGE III:
MASTERY

Stage III covers 500 most complex words in the English language. Much like Stage II, Stage III will provide you with a word list (plus their part of speech and meaning), fill-in-the-blank sentences, and a short passage. The words in Stage III were chosen by combing through standardised exams like AP English, ACT, and SAT tests from the past few years and picking out the most challenging words used. However, even if you don't plan on taking any standardised exam like the SAT's or ACT's, Stage III is still a vital part of improving your reading comprehension and enhancing your writing skills!

LESSON ONE

Target Words

1. Abhor
2. Abominate
3. Abridge
4. Abstruse
5. Abut
6. Abyss
7. Accolade
8. Adjunct
9. Affidavit
10. Affinity

LESSON ONE

A. Dictation

____ /10

B. Fill in the blanks with the most appropriate words

01 British Columbia _____ Alberta on its eastern border.

02 An _____ dictionary is one that has been shortened.

03 David _____ vegetables. He doesn't even want them off his dinner plate.

04 The defense lawyer had a sworn _____ from witnesses claiming his client was innocent of the crime charged against him.

05 Staring down the _____ of the mine shaft we were uncertain of how deep it was.

06 It is a fact that most people _____ the thought of public speaking.

07 A natural _____ exists between monkeys and apes.

08 After running in his first marathon, Mike said he didn't do it for the _____ he just wanted to get back in shape.

09 The library was an _____ to the Blakemore's original home.

10 Chemistry is an _____ subject of study for many students.

LESSON TWO

Target Words

1. Aftermath
2. Aggrandize
3. Ajar
4. Alienate
5. Alleviate
6. Allure
7. Aloof
8. Also-ran
9. Altercation
10. Alternative

LESSON TWO

A. Dictation

____ /10

B. Fill in the blanks with the most appropriate words

01 Barb was _____ from her group when they learned that she was the town gossip.

02 Tired of always being an _____, Mike trained hard and finally won the annual club tennis tournament.

03 To _____ his achievements Richard would make up unbelievable stories of personal accomplishments.

04 When the pitcher hit the batter with a fastball an _____ soon broke out between both teams.

05 The actress _____ the crowd with her overwhelming beauty.

06 An_____ of the bombing of Hiroshima was thousands of cancer cases caused by radiation.

07 The _____ to playing in the band was to go out for the football team

08 By leaving the front door of the house _____, hundreds of mosquitoes kept me awake all night long.

09 At the wedding reception, the bride's relatives were very _____, hardly speaking to the groom's guests and family.

10 Aspirin _____ painful headaches most of the time.

LESSON THREE

Target Words

1. Ambiance
2. Amiable
3. Amplify
4. Antecedent
5. Anterior
6. Appalling
7. Aptitude
8. Archaic
9. Arduous
10. Artisan

LESSON THREE

A. Dictation

____ /10

B. Fill in the blanks with the most appropriate words

01 The steam engine was the _____ to the gasoline engine.

02 The _____ in the Italian restaurant was delightful, there was soft music, candlelight, and singing waiters.

03 Laura has an _____ for numbers; ever since she was young, she always received high marks in math class.

04 The _____ young man helped the old lady carry her groceries to her car.

05 The _____ of Pueblo, Mexico are known for their beautiful pottery.

06 The assignment given the recruits was an _____ twenty-mile hike with full packs in the hot sun.

07 The _____ position of a ship is called the bow.

08 The music was _____ to the point where the guests couldn't hear themselves speak.

09 Underdeveloped countries that depend on agriculture for their economy will never raise their standard of living as long as they use _____ farm tools.

10 Karen had an _____ look on her face after seeing the destruction the hurricane had caused to her house.

LESSON FOUR

Target Words

1. Askew
2. Aspire
3. Assuage
4. Astute
5. Asunder
6. Atrophy
7. Atypical
8. Austere
9. Badger
10. Ballistics

LESSON FOUR

A. Dictation

____ /10

B. Fill in the blanks with the most appropriate words

01 Tim _____ to be the valedictorian of his class at graduation and studied hard to reach that goal.

02 Mike's _____ dorm room only had one chair and a mattress.

03 The curtains had been drawn _____.

04 A banana without a curve in its length is _____ of the species.

05 Many athletes drink sport drinks to _____ their thirst.

06 I hate to be _____ by phone solicitors.

07 The tire wouldn't fit on the car because in the accident the axle had been bent _____.

08 Mary was known to be very _____. She was always the first to finish her assignments.

09 Detective Culleton specializes in _____ and is always called to a crime scene whenever a firearm is involved.

10 The _____ bodies of the starving children were an appalling sight.

LESSON FIVE

Target Words

1. Balm
2. Beget
3. Beleaguer
4. Bereave
5. Beset
6. Bizarre
7. Blather
8. Bleak
9. Bludgeon
10. Bucolic

LESSON FIVE

A. Dictation

_____ /10

B. Fill in the blanks with the most appropriate words

01 All Mary likes to do is _____ with her friends on the phone.

02 "Wasn't he _____?" Lorna said of the strange man who appeared from nowhere and offered her an apple.

03 The _____ widow wore a black dress to her husband's funeral.

04 It was a _____ day, perfect for a game of golf or a trip to the beach.

05 The detective suspected the murder weapon was some type of _____.

06 Mr. Pride's farm with its peaceful green pastures and a babbling brook, was the perfect _____ setting for a picnic.

07 The game looked _____ with our team being down 42 to 7 in the fourth quarter.

08 during his last year in office, Richard Nixon was a _____ president, struggling to fight off the Watergate scandal.

09 Prior to the development of large farm machinery, farmers used to _____ large families to help them run their farms.

10 The losing team was _____ with disappointment.

LESSON SIX

Target Words

1. Bulwark
2. Cache
3. Cacophony
4. Cajole
5. Callous
6. Callow
7. Candour (US Candor)
8. Capacious
9. Castigate
10. Catapult

LESSON SIX

A. Dictation

____ /10

B. Fill in the blanks with the most appropriate words

01 The old castle has a _____ dining room large enough to seat a small army.

02 The _____ boater did not have a life preserver, paddle, or radio onboard his sailboat.

03 Jeannie always sweet-talked and _____ her parents into letting her have her way.

04 . Jimmy's mother _____ him for tracking mud on their new living room carpet.

05 . The police uncovered a _____ of weapons and money at the gang's hideout.

06 Without regard to feelings, our teacher said she would criticize our term papers with absolute _____.

07 An unpleasant _____ of sound was produced as the orchestra tuned their instruments. But once they began to play together the sounds became euphonious.

08 . When the Dolphins beat the Steelers, the victory_____ them into first place.

09 The _____ movie star would not sign autographs or even acknowledge her fans.

10 Quebec City is the only city in North America with a _____ built entirely around it.

LESSON SEVEN

Target Words

1. Catharsis
2. Caucus
3. Cerebral
4. Certify
5. Chasm
6. Chattel
7. Chide
8. Chronic
9. Circa
10. Citadel

LESSON SEVEN

A. Dictation

_____ /10

B. Fill in the blanks with the most appropriate words

01 The _____ young man received a perfect score on his SAT test.

02 When lower back pain becomes _____, it's time to see a doctor.

03 Getting out of the city and going to the mountains is Chuck's annual_____.

04 The _____ belonging to Herodotos of Athens at his death were sixteen slaves, seven horses, six hunting dogs, and three dwarf gladiators.

05 When Bobby threw his toys against the wall, his father _____ him for his bad temper.

06 During the monthly _____, the senator from Florida brought up the issue of runaway insurance rate hikes.

07 The exact date of the first Egyptian dynasty is not known, but it is believed to have occurred _____ 3000 BC.

08 The valuable papers arrived by _____ mail.

09 There are many ancient _____ in Spain, they are among the attractions most visited by tourists.

10 We crossed the huge _____ on a flimsy rope bridge.

LESSON EIGHT

Target Words

1. Claimant
2. Cloister
3. Commodious
4. Comprise
5. Congenial
6. Connoisseur
7. Consensus
8. Coterie
9. Countenance
10. Coup

LESSON EIGHT

A. Dictation

____ /10

B. Fill in the blanks with the most appropriate words

01 The _____ limousine accommodated the entire family and our luggage.

02 The judge awarded all six of the _____ an equal share of the insurance money.

03 The first aid kit was _____ of a bottle of aspirin, two gauze pads, and a pair of scissors.

04 The family _____ was to celebrate Christmas at Aunt Karen's house this year.

05 The _____ Dr. Armstrong always had a smile and a kind word for his patients, and candies for the children.

06 Rock stars have a _____ of fans who follow them around like leeches.

07 The submarine commander's _____ belied his true feelings of anxiety and fear.

08 The violent _____ ended when the radical political leaders were escorted out of the capitol in shackles.

09 Mary regarded her sewing room as a _____ where she could withdraw from her hectic life as a mother of six and enjoy moments of privacy.

10 My uncle is a _____ of fine wines.

LESSON NINE

Target Words

1. Couture
2. Cower
3. Cranny
4. Craven
5. Creditor
6. Criterion
7. Cubism
8. Curtail
9. Curvilinear
10. Damper

LESSON NINE

A. Dictation

____ /10

B. Fill in the blanks with the most appropriate words

01 When Sheriff Wild Bill Hickok entered the Last Chance Saloon, the villains _____ in fear.

02 The unexpected rain put a _____ on plans to have a picnic at the beach.

03 Rock climbers look for any _____ where they can get a secure foothold.

04 Mike's knee injury _____ his career as a professional football player.

05 Pablo Picasso did not originate _____, but he is credited with popularizing it.

06 The fashion model walked the runway wearing the latest _____.

07 Engineers have special instruments to lay out _____ streets in subdivisions.

08 Visa, Master Card, and American Express companies are _____.

09 The _____ for becoming a lawyer is graduating from law school and passing the state bar exam.

10 The soldier was full of bluster about how bravely he would fight, but his comrades later found him to be _____.

LESSON TEN

Target Words

1. Dauntless
2. Dearth
3. Debacle
4. Debase
5. Decree
6. Deduce
7. Defame
8. Deft
9. Demagogue
10. Demonic

LESSON TEN

A. Dictation

____/10

B. Fill in the blanks with the most appropriate words

01 In one _____ move, the policeman subdued the thief and took him to the ground.

02 The _____ soldier attacked the enemy line with no regard to the machine gun fire and mortar rounds exploding all around him.

03 Walter had a _____ approach to business; he was only out there for himself and the money.

04 A _____ of rain last summer led to many failed crops, especially corn and cotton in the valley.

05 Avid smokers protested the _____ which prohibits smoking in all restaurants and public buildings.

06 Historians will almost exclusively agree that Hitler and Mussolini were _____ who were greatly responsible for starting World War II.

07 False accusations by lying men have _____ the reputations of many reputable women.

08 Inflation in Brazil has _____ the value of money so much that people won't stoop to recover small coins in the street.

09 It was an absolute _____ for Agassi as he lost the third set without winning a single point.

10 The detective _____ that the killer's weapon was a knife based on the wounds left on the victim.

LESSON ELEVEN

Target Words

1. Demur
2. Denounce
3. Desiccate
4. Dilemma
5. Disparage
6. Dispel
7. Disperse
8. Dissolution
9. Divine
10. Docile

LESSON ELEVEN

A. Dictation

____ /10

B. Fill in the blanks with the most appropriate words

01. The drought was the worst in fifty years, and the oranges on the trees were _____.

02. The _____ of their marriage was caused by Stan's infidelity.

03. The police arrived to _____ the raging crowd with threats of arrest if they did not leave the parade grounds.

04. At the press conference, the irate coach _____ the referees for all the bad calls he thought he received.

05. Jealousy made Ellen make many _____ remarks about Rachel's prom dress.

06. My parents told us to _____ any notions of inviting a bunch of friends over to the house and having a wild party while they were gone for the weekend.

07. John faced the _____ of either taking a cut in pay or losing his job.

08. The _____ dolphin was easily approached by its new trainer.

09. Stockbrokers make their living helping their clients _____ when to buy and when to sell stocks.

10. The mayor said he would _____ if asked to speak at the town rally.

LESSON TWELVE

Target Words

1. Doldrums
2. Domain
3. Dormant
4. Draconian
5. Dromedary
6. Dulcet
7. Duress
8. Edifice
9. Efface
10. Egalitarian

LESSON TWELVE

A. Dictation

____ /10

B. Fill in the blanks with the most appropriate words

01 The crew was under _____ after drifting for three days in a rubber raft with no food or water.

02 The _____ of the native Florida panther is in the Everglades and South Central Florida.

03 Ever since Jackie's dog died, he hasn't touched his toys and moped around day after day in the _____.

04 The _____ music in the elevator made the ride to the fifty-fifth floor pleasurable.

05 Bears hibernate in caves and remain _____ throughout the winter.

06 It was hard to make out the old coin's date because it had been _____ over time.

07 Martin Luther King was a true _____; he preached for equal rights for all citizens.

08 The construction of one _____ led to another, and New York City became a skyline of enormous skyscrapers.

09 The highlight of our trip to Egypt was riding _____ around the Great Pyramids of Giza.

10 Our _____ professor always gives us at least three hours of homework a night and term papers to write over every holiday.

LESSON THIRTEEN

Target Words

1. Elapse
2. Elfin
3. Embellish
4. Embody
5. Emit
6. Emulate
7. Endure
8. Engulf
9. Enrage
10. Enrapture

LESSON THIRTEEN

A. Dictation

____ /10

B. Fill in the blanks with the most appropriate words

01 The sleeping dog _____ a groan which startled us.

02 Settlers in the 1800s _____ many hardships on their way to California.

03 The _____ character of Tinkerbell in the Walt Disney movie Peter Pan will always be remembered by generations of Disney fans.

04 The hurricane completely _____ the town in a surge of wind and water.

05 Two years _____ before they were to meet again, but all the time Jonathan knew Annette was the girl he was going to marry.

06 The famous golfer, Tiger Woods, has a golf swing that many golfers try to _____.

07 The crowd became _____ when it was announced that the concert had been cancelled.

08 Eric _____ his fishing stories; you would think his catches were as big as whales.

09 The kids were _____ with the idea of taking the day off from school and going to Disney World.

10 Michael Jordan _____ all the attributes of being a hall of fame basketball player and sports legend.

LESSON FOURTEEN

Target Words

1. Ensemble
2. Entice
3. Entomb
4. Entomology
5. Entreat
6. Erudite
7. Euphonious
8. Evade
9. Evoke
10. Exhume

LESSON FOURTEEN

A. Dictation

____/10

B. Fill in the blanks with the most appropriate words

01 The escaped prisoners _____ the authorities by breaking into a church and disguising themselves as nuns.

02 Grandpa tried to _____ a smile from the baby by tickling her chin.

03 The delicious aroma of popcorn in the theater lobby _____ us to purchase a large bucket before the movie.

04 The judge issued a court order to _____ the grave of an unknown soldier.

05 Carly sings in the choir because she has a sweet, _____ voice.

06 When mom was diagnosed with cancer, we searched for the most _____ doctor we could find.

07 The primary function of _____ is to discover how to prevent insects from destroying crops.

08 Darla found the perfect pair of shoes to match her _____ she is going to wear to the prom.

09 Our entire family _____ our father to take us on a summer vacation to Europe.

10 The Egyptians _____ their kings in special burial chambers together with all their possessions needed in the afterlife.

LESSON FIFTEEN

Target Words

1. Expunge
2. Facilitate
3. Fathom
4. Fawn
5. Feign
6. Fester
7. Fetish
8. Fickle
9. Fjord
10. Fleece

LESSON FIFTEEN

A. Dictation

____ /10

B. Fill in the blanks with the most appropriate words

01 The housewives on our street were _____ by a con man selling bogus magazine subscriptions.

02 Brad is a _____ eater; it's hard to say what he likes to eat.

03 The grandmother _____ over her grandchild, tickling him and making goo-goo sounds.

04 The wet and muddy footprints were _____ with soap and water.

05 In order to _____ the sale of their home, George came down on the price.

06 Mary has a _____ for chocolate, she hides a box under her bed, in her desk at the office, and in her purse.

07 The jury found it hard to _____ how the defendant could commit such a terrible crime.

08 Elizabeth _____ illness in order to stay home from school on the day of her final exam.

09 Diane's _____ resentments toward her boss finally drove her to quit her job.

10 Norway and New Zealand are two countries noted for having the most scenic _____ in the world.

LESSON SIXTEEN

Target Words

1. Forage
2. Forbear
3. Forsake
4. Fortuitous
5. Fraught
6. Gamin
7. Gazebo
8. Generalize
9. Giddy
10. Girdle

LESSON SIXTEEN

A. Dictation

____ /10

B. Fill in the blanks with the most appropriate words

01 After Sue won the beauty contest, she was absolutely _____ with joy.

02 After the campers fell asleep in their tents, the raccoons began _____ through the camp site for anything to eat.

03 Kathy was _____ with guilt about losing her temper with the children when she found out it wasn't their fault.

04 Our teacher asked us to be specific when answering the test questions and avoid _____.

05 My dad always told me to stay in school and study hard or I'd become a _____.

06 On Sunday afternoons the family would gather together in the shade of our backyard _____.

07 It was _____ missing the ill-fated flight because of the traffic jam on the way to the airport.

08 It is lovely to spend time in my grandma's garden that is _____ by oak trees.

09 Sally said it was difficult to _____ smoking after doing it for twenty years.

10 The parents urged their daughter to _____ her career as a model and return to their home to become a school teacher.

LESSON SEVENTEEN

Target Words

1. Girth
2. Gloat
3. Glutton
4. Gossamer
5. Grandiloquent
6. Grandiose
7. Guile
8. Guise
9. Harangue
10. Harrowing

LESSON SEVENTEEN

A. Dictation

____ /10

B. Fill in the blanks with the most appropriate words

01 The _____ shawl she wore was not enough to keep her warm in the frigid air.

02 The undercover police car had the _____ of a typical family car.

03 The _____ of the ticket scalper was shocking. He was selling tickets today for yesterday's tennis matches.

04 The neighbor's kids are such _____, whenever they come over they clean out the fridge.

05 The _____ of the planet Earth is about twenty-five thousand miles.

06 After winning the state championship last year, the football team _____ for a whole year until they lost the first game of the season

07 They may be eloquent, but there is nothing grand about pompous _____ speakers.

08 After the _____ experience when Eddie's main parachute didn't open, and his emergency chute saved him only at the last minute, he vowed never to jump again.

09 The sergeant _____ his recruits for not keeping in step as the platoon practiced marching.

10 The director demanded a _____ car chase in his action movie.

LESSON EIGHTEEN

Target Words

1. Herbicide
2. Histrionic
3. Hoard
4. Hovel
5. Husbandry
6. Idiosyncrasy
7. Impede
8. Incite
9. Incongruous
10. Infamy

LESSON EIGHTEEN

A. Dictation

____/10

B. Fill in the blanks with the most appropriate words

01 Stan's _____ of constantly clicking his pen drove the whole class crazy.

02 The poor live in _____ on the outskirts of town.

03 Waving a stick at Jerry's dog only _____ him and increases the chance he will bite you.

04 Laura doesn't eat her Halloween candy; instead, she likes to _____ it and make it last all year.

05 The great white shark has been made _____ by the movie Jaws.

06 Ed appeared _____ wearing his tuxedo on an old-fashioned hayride.

07 The young actor's _____ portrayal of his character was too much to bear.

08 Bud's superb _____ of his orange grove resulted in a larger than expected crop this year.

09 Many farmers use _____ for controlling weeds on their farms.

10 The bad weather _____ the climber's attempt to summit Mount Everest by nightfall.

LESSON NINETEEN

Target Words

1. Insouciant
2. Intervene
3. Inveigle
4. Irascible
5. Joust
6. Karma
7. Laconic
8. Lament
9. Languish
10. Lassitude

LESSON NINETEEN

A. Dictation

____ /10

B. Fill in the blanks with the most appropriate words

01. It was a _____ to the death between Sir Lancelot and the Black Knight.

02. The school principal became so _____ even his teachers avoided speaking to him.

03. There must have been thousands of people at the funeral to _____ the death of Princess Diane.

04. Our teenage daughter doesn't like it when her mother and I _____ in her social life.

05. The president's _____ speech only lasted ten minutes, when it usually takes an hour.

06. Bob's _____ demeanor in the locker room before the big game meant he was extremely confident that we would win.

07. Laura _____ her history teacher into allowing her to retake the mid-term exam she missed because she overslept.

08. Running in his first marathon, Kevin began to _____ with only a mile to go.

09. _____ finally overcame the weary travelers after a full day of traveling.

10. Louise often told her friends it was her _____ to die young and beautiful.

LESSON TWENTY

Target Words

1. Laudable
2. Lax
3. Legacy
4. Lesion
5. Lethargy
6. Lexicon
7. Lieu
8. Loiter
9. Maim
10. Marauder

LESSON TWENTY

A. Dictation

____/10

B. Fill in the blanks with the most appropriate words

01 Among the legendary pirate _____ of the eighteenth century were Captain Kidd, Calico Jack Rackam, Charles Vane, Blackbeard, and Sir Henry Morgan.

02 It is against the rules to _____ on school grounds on the weekends.

03 Sailors have a nautical _____; " port means left, starboard means right, bow means front, and stern means rear."

04 The _____ of the copper mining industry is the creation of mountains of waste where beautiful, unspoiled forests once stood.

05 The _____ deer scurried into the woods after being wounded by the hunter's arrow.

06 The bank robbers planned to rob the bank when security was _____.

07 The president's _____ speech ended with a standing ovation.

08 In _____ of driving our own car to the restaurant, we decided to take a taxi.

09 Ebola is an infectious disease characterized by open _____ of the skin.

10 _____ overcame everyone after eating a huge Thanksgiving dinner.

LESSON TWENTY-ONE

Target Words

1. Marshal
2. Martyr
3. Masticate
4. Melancholy
5. Menagerie
6. Migratory
7. Milieu
8. Mirage
9. Misanthropy
10. Misnomer

LESSON TWENTY-ONE

A. Dictation

____ /10

B. Fill in the blanks with the most appropriate words

01 Desert caravans often see _____ on days when heat waves are reflected off the burning sands.

02 _____ their forces, the British defeated Rommel at El Alamein.

03 The New York Stock Exchange is a _____ of frenzied activity during trading hours.

04 Busch Gardens has a wonderful _____ of lions, tigers, elephants, and other wild animals roaming free and on display in a park-like setting.

05 A nickname like "Speedy" is a _____ when directed toward one who is slow at what they do.

06 The doctor explained that a person's digestion is aided when they _____ their food thoroughly.

07 Fruit pickers are _____ workers who move from place to place at harvesting time.

08 Joan of Arc was undoubtedly the most famous _____ in modern history, burned at the stake because she refused to go against her beliefs.

09 Adolph Hitler is known for his _____.

10 It was a _____ day, gloomy and dark.

LESSON TWENTY-TWO

Target Words

1. Mode
2. Mores
3. Muse
4. Muster
5. Myriad
6. Nepotism
7. Noisome
8. Noxious
9. Oblique
10. Obtuse

LESSON TWENTY-TWO

A. Dictation

___/10

B. Fill in the blanks with the most appropriate words

01 Dan _____ all his strength to lift the weight over his head.

02 The politician's _____ answers to the press's questions raised many questions about his integrity.

03 The players knew it was _____ when the coach named his son starting quarterback even though he was the worst player on the team.

04 Though the odds of winning the lottery are very low, it is fun to _____ about what you would do if you actually won.

05 After graduating from Harvard with a master's degree in business, Paul had a _____ of career opportunities ahead of him.

06 The _____ boy failed every class.

07 Once he became a lawyer, Hal put aside his jeans and dressed in the _____ of his contemporaries, conservative dark suits, white shirts, and ties.

08 The _____ pollutants discharged into the bay by the paper mill killed all the marine life.

09 According to Chinese _____, it is considered polite for dinner guests to belch at the table as a gesture of appreciation and enjoyment.

10 The comedian's act was absolutely _____; all of his jokes depended entirely on four-lettered words.

LESSON TWENTY-THREE

Target Words

1. Opportune
2. Optimum
3. Orthodox
4. Ostracize
5. Oust
6. Paradox
7. Paranoia
8. Parry
9. Partition
10. Penitent

LESSON TWENTY-THREE

A. Dictation

____/10

B. Fill in the blanks with the most appropriate words

01 He must have been pretty _____ to fall for that old trick.

02 Even when Jason turned 18, he was still rather _____ and needed to grow up.

03 Success in business comes not by understanding and meeting the demands of millions of _____ customers, but by cementing relationships with and winning the support of them.

04 To be perfectly _____ with you, I don't think she's the woman for the job.

05 More than 6,000 people took to the streets of Dublin at the weekend in a _____ and colourful celebration.

06 In my _____ opinion, we should never have bought that villa in the first place, my lord.

07 The _____ weather conditions made the mission extremely difficult.

08 We face the _____ prospect of still high unemployment.

09 I would be most _____ if you would send me the book immediately.

10 The opposition leader led a very _____ attack on the government in parliament this morning.

LESSON TWENTY-FOUR

Target Words

1. Periphery
2. Permeate
3. Perverse
4. Petulant
5. Philanthropy
6. Phobia
7. Photogenic
8. Pied
9. Pillage
10. Pique

LESSON TWENTY-FOUR

A. Dictation

____ /10

B. Fill in the blanks with the most appropriate words

01 The _____ young actress posed for photographers in front of her awaiting limousine.

02 Colonel Mason posted guards at the _____ of the camp for night security.

03 The _____ old man sat on his porch and yelled at us for walking across his lawn.

04 The _____ referee would not change his call even though the replay showed he was wrong.

05 Football star Warrick Dunn is also known for his _____; he helps underprivileged families own their own homes.

06 Before the explosion, witnesses said the smell of gasoline _____ the flight cabin.

07 The sound of the car horn _____ our curiosity until we saw our neighbor had accidently pressed it while backing out of his driveway.

08 The _____ horse was easy to spot in the race.

09 The enemy invaders _____ the village, taking everything not tied down and killing the cows and chickens.

10 Those who have a _____ about heights are said to be acrophobic.

LESSON TWENTY-FIVE

Target Words

1. Plight
2. Porcine
3. Potentate
4. Precarious
5. Procrastinate
6. Proficient
7. Propulsive
8. Prowess
9. Quandary
10. Queue

LESSON TWENTY-FIVE

A. Dictation

____ /10

B. Fill in the blanks with the most appropriate words

01 Because of his _____ in battle, Brad was awarded the silver star.

02 Laura received a bad grade on her science project because she _____ finishing it until the day before it was due.

03 The _____ at Disney World are usually the longest during holiday weekends.

04 John was scared to climb the _____ ladder because he didn't want to fall and break his back.

05 Andrea was in a _____. She was asked to the prom by two boys she really liked.

06 Ever since Sarah was elected president of the junior class, she walks around with her nose in the air, as if she thinks she is a _____.

07 The _____ force of a nuclear submarine is superior to the older diesel powered submarines.

08 In order to endure the _____ smell of the pigsty, Frank tied a bandana around his head to cover his nose.

09 Wally was the most _____ tennis player in our league, but he wasn't good enough to win the regional tournament.

10 Determined to rescue the fifty hostages from their _____, the police rushed the aircraft before the terrorists could cause further harm.

LESSON TWENTY-SIX

Target Words

1. Quirk
2. Quixotic
3. Ramification
4. Relinquish
5. Reminisce
6. Remorse
7. Resurgent
8. Revere
9. Rivet
10. Roster

LESSON TWENTY-SIX

A. Dictation

____ /10

B. Fill in the blanks with the most appropriate words

01 John refused to feel any _____ for doing what he considered the right thing to do.

02 The _____ of not studying for a test is the high probability of failing it.

03 The football program has a _____ for both teams with the player's jersey numbers and positions.

04 Watch out for this horse's _____; he bucks every time he sneezes.

05 Sally's _____ dream was that a prince riding a white stallion would someday scoop her up and ask her to marry him.

06 The home crowd was _____ as their player stood at the foul line ready to shoot the winning basket.

07 Bobby would not _____ his bag of Halloween candy and fell asleep with it clutched in his arms.

08 After failing math the last two years, the _____ young boy studied diligently and passed with an A.

09 After my mother died, it was hard not to _____ about all the great times we had together.

10 Mother Teresa was greatly _____ by all who knew of her humanitarian work in Africa.

61

LESSON TWENTY-SEVEN

Target Words

1. Rudimentary
2. Scapegoat
3. Scrutinize
4. Segregate
5. Serpentine
6. Sombre (US Somber)
7. Sonorous
8. Spur
9. Spurn
10. Stupefy

LESSON TWENTY-SEVEN

A. Dictation

____/10

B. Fill in the blanks with the most appropriate words

01 The _____ race track was a challenging course for the drivers, especially in the rain.

02 The cattleman built a fence to _____ the bulls from the heifers.

03 The _____ weather forecast spoiled our weekend plans to go to the beach.

04 Each soldier's uniform is _____ by his commanding officer.

05 I told Sam that I wasn't going to be his _____; he was the one who broke the window, not me.

06 John Barrymore's _____ voice enraptured audiences across the land for decades.

07 The magician's trick left his audience _____.

08 The buyer's ridiculously low offer to buy the house was _____ by the seller.

09 The eating utensils and tools of early cave dwellers during the Ice Age were very _____ _____.

10 The general _____ his troops to make one last effort to take the hill.

LESSON TWENTY-EIGHT

Target Words

1. Sundry
2. Supplant
3. Surfeit
4. Tether
5. Torque
6. Trenchant
7. Truculent
8. Truncate
9. Tyro
10. Ubiquitous

LESSON TWENTY-EIGHT

A. Dictation

____ /10

B. Fill in the blanks with the most appropriate words

01. We _____ the boat to the dock with lines both fore and aft.

02. The wrench handle was too short to generate the _____ required to loosen the bolt.

03. Because of unforeseen circumstances, our vacation was _____ after the first week.

04. There was a _____ of delicious food at the family picnic.

05. A _____ store is usually like a five and dime, a store carrying a variety of miscellaneous items for the household and personal use

06. After the starting quarterback threw three interceptions in the first half, the coach _____ _____ him with the second string quarterback in the second half.

07. Julia had a _____ tongue and was always putting her friends down behind their backs.

08. The marine recruits were scolded by their _____ sergeant for any small offense.

09. Computers were once rare, but today are more _____ than typewriters.

10. When it comes to cooking, Bob is such a _____. He can't even boil water without making a mess.

LESSON TWENTY-NINE

Target Words

1. Umbrage
2. Unbridled
3. Veer
4. Verbatim
5. Vertigo
6. Volition
7. Wane
8. Wither
9. Wrest
10. Wrath

LESSON TWENTY-NINE

A. Dictation

____/10

B. Fill in the blanks with the most appropriate words

01 Poly, the parrot, will repeat whatever is said to him _____.

02 The crop _____ from the lack of rain.

03 Police with tell you that in dealing with a person who threatens you with a knife or a club, it is the best policy not to attempt to _____ the weapon away from them.

04 Andrea's _____ passion for dancing was evident in every performance she gave.

05 Dad said he couldn't ride any of the amusement park rides that spin because they gave him _____.

06 Without warning, Flight #638 suddenly _____ off the runway and slammed into a small plane parked outside the hangar.

07 Did you really want to incur her _____ when she is known for inflicting the worst punishments legally possible?

08 Polly took _____ when her husband told her she was wearing too much makeup and looked older than she was by trying to look younger than she was.

09 Dave decided to join the Army of his own _____ in lieu of going to college.

10 A _____ interest by theatre-goers prompted the theater to shut down.

LESSON THIRTY

Target Words

1. Wanton
2. Wily
3. Winsome
4. Wistful
5. Wizened
6. Yoke
7. Yore
8. Zealous
9. Zenith
10. Zephyr

LESSON THIRTY

A. Dictation

_____ /10

B. Fill in the blanks with the most appropriate words

01. Since her pet rabbit died, Edda missed it terribly and sat around _____ all day long.

02. After such a long, frustrating day, I was grateful for Chris's _____ attitude and childish naiveté.

03. Agatha's grandmother, Stephanie, had the most _____ countenance, full of leathery wrinkles

04. We _____ together the logs by tying a string around them.

05. I was too nice to tell Nelly that she had reached the absolute _____ of her career with that one hit of hers.

06. If not for the _____ that were blowing and cooling us, our room would've been unbearably hot.

07. In the days of _____ we didn't have the luxuries of air-conditioning, televisions and home computers.

08. Vicky's _____ demeanor often made the frat guys next door very excited.

09. Though they were not the strongest of the Thundercats, _____ Kit and Kat were definitely the most clever and full of tricks.

10. If he were any more _____ about getting his promotion, he'd practically live at the office.

LESSON ONE

Target Words

1. Abhor
2. Abominate
3. Abridge
4. Abstruse
5. Abut
6. Abyss
7. Accolade
8. Adjunct
9. Affidavit
10. Affinity

A. Fill in the blanks with the most appropriate words.

01. My mother likes to buy Reader's Digest versions of books. She prefers the _____ versions of novels because she is too busy to read full-sized books.

02. As the cruise ship travelled through the night, the ocean passing below was like a dark, churning _____.

03. The tennis champion was awarded many _____ for his winning performance in the game.

04. Though many may not choose to pursue a career in computers, those classes are still an _____ course for engineering majors.

05. She was terrified of heights and therefore _____ the idea of going parasailing.

06. I took a break from my physics homework because of the _____ content of the chapter I'd been reading.

07. He has an _____ for all things horror; his room is decorated with scary movie posters, and he loves to read books by Stephen King.

08. The judge demanded an _____ from the defense attorney.

09. We parked in a space _____ the grocery store.

10. Most people _____ those who abuse animals, and rightly so!

LESSON ONE

B. Fill in the blanks in the passage with the most appropriate words.
Passage 1:

Professor Spinet had an _____ for intellectual pursuits. She worked as an _____ teacher for years before finally earning the _____ of a teaching job at the local university. Most days she found herself getting lost within the _____ of books in the library, where she could spend hours reading _____ research papers and hefty, one thousand-page novels—never the _____ versions! One day, she noticed a student sitting at a desk _____ her own by the study carrels. The student was reading a law book and seemed to be studying. Just then, the student looked around and suddenly ripped out a page from the book! Professor Spinet absolutely _____ people who damaged books, especially ones that didn't belong to them!

She was usually very non-confrontational, but as a professor of the university she felt a responsibility to reprimand the student. Plus, she knew she would _____ herself if she didn't speak up! Professor Spinet went over to the student and tapped him on the shoulder. The student looked up guiltily and knew he had been caught. Spinet told him that he would need to pay for a replacement book. Though she didn't acquire a signed _____ stating his guilt, she thought that making him shell out the money to replace the book he had defaced was justice enough.

LESSON TWO

Target Words

1. Aftermath
2. Aggrandize
3. Ajar
4. Alienate
5. Alleviate
6. Allure
7. Aloof
8. Also-ran
9. Altercation
10. Alternative

A. Fill in the blanks with the most appropriate words.

01. Her bedroom grew cold because she accidentally left the window _____.

02. After tripping and falling in front of the entire school during the talent show, Mindy couldn't help but feel _____ from everyone the entire week after.

03. There is an undeniable _____ surrounding the island of Fiji. Its beauty is legendary.

04. The car behind us ran into our bumper at a stoplight. My father was furious, and soon an _____ erupted between him and the driver who had hit his vehicle.

05. She was extremely _____ throughout the whole party, and it wasn't until later that I realized it was because she didn't know anyone besides the host.

06. Crystal healing is a kind of _____ medicine whose benefits are widely disputed between scientists and practitioners alike.

07. The worst of the hurricane was surely the _____. People were left without power, clean water, and, in extreme cases, their homes.

08. He hoped that by running for student body president, he could _____ his reputation.

09. She _____ her mosquito bite by rubbing ice on the inflamed, itchy area.

10. No one would call the wrestler an _____ because most of them believed he was simply down on his luck.

LESSON TWO

B. Fill in the blanks in the passage with the most appropriate words.
Passage 2:

In the _____ of his skiing accident, Terrence felt only lethargic and reclusive. His catastrophic blunder had left him with two broken legs, and he had been in the hospital for over three weeks. Being there made him feel _____. Perhaps it was the window in his room, which was never left _____ due to the icy weather outside. Despite the lack of fresh air, a number of friends came to visit him. They had wished him well, hoping to _____ his loneliness and depression, but he still had trouble talking to them. Even his family noticed Terrence acting somewhat _____, so they began to brainstorm _____ ways to get him back to his old self.

A week after Terrence's first surgery, he began physical therapy. One of his therapy nurses was an older woman with a lot of attitude and determination. Terrence was worried she might be too brassy and cause an _____, but to his surprise everyone found her _____! Still feeling like an _____ in a race, Terrence avoided speaking with her as much as he could. But physical therapy was hard work, and it wasn't long before his audacious physical therapy nurse was cheering Terrence on as he took his first steps in nearly a month. As she cheered, Terrence smiled and carried on, his self-confidence slowly _____, all due to this unabashed woman and his own willpower.

LESSON THREE

Target Words

1. Ambiance
2. Amiable
3. Amplify
4. Antecedent
5. Anterior
6. Appalling
7. Aptitude
8. Archaic
9. Arduous
10. Artisan

A. Fill in the blanks with the most appropriate words.

01. Many _____ gather to sell their wares at the local arts and crafts festival.

02. She hated going to the grocery store because it always seemed like such an _____ task.

03. There are four _____ vital cardiac veins in the heart.

04. The lute could be considered the _____ to the modern acoustic guitar.

05. That year, the party planning committee decided to imbue the Halloween gala with a carnival _____.

06. The academic program requires incoming students take an _____ test to determine their qualifications.

07. The look on his face said it all: he thought her dress was _____.

08. Though Latin is said to be a dead, _____ language, there can be no doubt that its linguistic influence remains ubiquitous.

09. Everyone loved Eva because she was such an _____ young girl.

10. Speakerphones are used to _____ the volume of someone's voice.

LESSON THREE

B. Fill in the blanks in the passage with the most appropriate words.
Passage 3:

Sara and Kevin had worked hard to make sure their wedding would be perfect. They were hoping to establish a certain _____ at the wedding. Their _____ wedding planner, a woman named Ella, specialized in themed weddings. This qualifying _____ was a major selling point for Sara and Kevin, who wanted to have a fantasy-themed wedding. Ella, a true _____ when it came to wedding planning, took every single one of their hopes to heart when determining _____ decorations in the church, food at the reception, music, invitations, and flower arrangements.

Her _____ for multitasking was impressive too! Despite the sheer number of _____ details involved in her job, she was always optimistic. She reasoned that if a wedding planner had an _____ and impatient attitude, that negativity would permeate everything when things finally came together. Instead, she chose to be as chipper and excited as could be. Her enthusiasm for her job _____ whenever she had a particularly challenging wedding to plan. She thought weddings were strange, wonderful, _____ events that were centers of love, happiness, and family, and she was only too glad to help others plan their own.

LESSON FOUR

Target Words

1. Askew
2. Aspire
3. Assuage
4. Astute
5. Asunder
6. Atrophy
7. Atypical
8. Austere
9. Badger
10. Ballistics

A. Fill in the blanks with the most appropriate words.

01. Being left-handed is now considered an _____ trait in humans.

02. She was a very _____-looking woman: her hair was tied back in a tight bun, and she had very sharp features.

03. The _____ team was called in to dismantle the bomb.

04. She threw her phone at the wall in anger, and it knocked the painting _____.

05. Davie _____ to be an astronaut when he grows up.

06. The prosecuting attorney's _____ observations led to the defendant being convicted for his heinous crimes.

07. Now is not the time for us to be torn _____ by trivial matters. We must unite against our common enemy!

08. His musical talents _____ from lack of regular practice.

09. I was hoping to _____ my younger brother's aversion towards doing my chores for me.

10. The protesters _____ the store employees to the point that they closed the shop for the day!

LESSON FOUR

B. Fill in the blanks in the passage with the most appropriate words.
Passage 4:

Jerry was undeniably clumsy. He could rarely go a single day without knocking things _____. He didn't know why he was so prone to clumsiness, but he _____ to be a more careful, poised person. In an attempt to be steadier and more self-aware, he started meditating. It was an _____ approach, and he found it difficult at first. Though clumsy, he was a surprisingly _____ man who did not joke often, and his lack of coordination made him go _____ on occasion. And, truth be told, his wife _____ his resistance towards trying meditation to cure his ungainliness. He didn't want her to continue _____ him about giving it a shot, so at last he gave in.

Eventually though, meditating began to catch on. He found himself becoming more _____ in his observations, and overall more conscious of the way he moved. Two months later, he rarely ever knocked things over, or found glassware broken _____. His clumsiness had _____, and he had finally transformed into the balanced, thoughtful person he so desired to become.

LESSON FIVE

Target Words

1. Balm
2. Beget
3. Beleaguer
4. Bereave
5. Beset
6. Bizarre
7. Blather
8. Bleak
9. Bludgeon
10. Bucolic

A. Fill in the blanks with the most appropriate words.

01 Her knuckles were chapped, so she rubbed _____ on them to moisturize her flaking, red skin.

02 The _____ parents had not been into their late son's room since his funeral.

03 I hate listening to people _____ about the latest, sensationalistic gossip.

04 The forecast was _____: the weatherman called for rain for the next ten days.

05 _____ with worries about the test the next day, she decided to call off her plans and stay home to study.

06 A pumpkin lay smashed in the street. Teenagers had _____ the rotting gourd to the point that its carved jack-o'-lantern face was no longer distinguishable.

07 They decided to move out of the big city and into a rural, _____ region of the country.

08 The actor, _____ with doubts about the seriousness of the role he had been offered, decided not to accept the part.

09 His mother keeps bugging him about when he will get married and _____ a few children to carry on the family name.

10 The play was so _____ that I couldn't tell whether or not I had enjoyed it!

LESSON FIVE

B. Fill in the blanks in the passage with the most appropriate words.
Passage 5:

The _____ scientist felt the weight of the world on his shoulders. _____ with problems concerning climate change, he felt useless in a world slowly being poisoned by its own doings. Though he had not yet had the chance in life to _____ any children of his own, he felt responsible for the health and safety of future generations and hoped they would not end up _____ by the devastation older generations had brought upon the planet's ecosystem. _____ by guilt and feeling heavily responsible for helping to solve the problems of the world, he worked with a team of researchers to spread clean energy.

The scientist had witnessed climate change firsthand. He lived in a _____ part of the country known for mild summers, _____ autumn and spring seasons, and snowy winters. But due to the steadily rising temperature of the earth's ozone, mild summers had become sweltering while snowy winters were now _____ and rainy with no sign of snow. This _____ change in the weather in his own hometown was enough to make him _____ to friends, families, and anyone else who would listen as he cautioned against the everlasting effects of global warming. It was a frightening prospect that they might never see winter again in their town, but it was enough to get the citizens concerned and involved.

LESSON SIX

Target Words

1. Bulwark
2. Cache
3. Cacophony
4. Cajole
5. Callous
6. Callow
7. Candour (US Candor)
8. Capacious
9. Castigate
10. Catapult

A. Fill in the blanks with the most appropriate words.

01. Though he used to be afraid of dogs, his girlfriend _____ him into getting one, and now he loves them!

02. Bobby's new car was the most _____, so we took that one on our road trip.

03. He was _____ to fame after winning an Oscar for Best Actor.

04. Somewhere in the attic is a _____ of old winter clothes.

05. It was just a mistake! Don't _____ him too harshly!

06. New York City is constantly abuzz with the _____ of urban living.

07. She was _____ enough to laugh at my sudden misfortune.

08. The political candidate's _____ and charm won everyone over.

09. They would never admit to being _____ when it came to programming, but I knew how inexperienced they really were.

10. The ancient _____ came crumbling down nearly four hundred years ago. Now it is a tourist attraction.

LESSON SIX

B. Fill in the blanks in the passage with the most appropriate words.
Passage 6:

The _____ had stood for nearly five hundred years, but it was finally beginning to show signs of age. Tina, one of the tour guides who regularly brought tourists to the attraction, was very protective of the _____ structure, and regularly had to _____ tourists who did not follow the rules or created a _____ of unwanted noise. She could remember one time in particular when an especially _____ group of tourists came to see it, and she had to _____ the group into following the rules seemingly every other minute.

Regardless of the seriousness with which she regarded her job, she was one of the best tour guides around. Her _____ and know-how won people over, and she made sure that even the most _____ tourists left the exhibit with new knowledge. She especially loved showing people the _____ that had once been used as a military defense against invading forces. There was even an arms _____ beneath it that had once stored other weapons! This facet of the attraction always created such a mix of excitement and reverence among the tourists, which only reminded Tina of how fortunate she was to have her job. She loved sharing the rich history of the place, and seeing their excitement was just another upside of that!

LESSON SEVEN

Target Words

1. Catharsis
2. Caucus
3. Cerebral
4. Certify
5. Chasm
6. Chattel
7. Chide
8. Chronic
9. Circa
10. Citadel

A. Fill in the blanks with the most appropriate words.

01. The _____ was too long to go around. We would have to find a way to cross it.

02. The teacher _____ her students after they answered the question incorrectly.

03. The _____ is an architect's dream. The structure utilizes various elegant styles of construction.

04. I have _____ insomnia, so I take a melatonin supplement before bed each night.

05. Hairstylists usually have to be _____ by a beauty school or other reputable institution.

06. Yoga is a _____ form of exercise that many people turn to for stress management.

07. The town _____ would be held in two weeks, and the man running for senator was nervous about the outcome!

08. The movie was a _____ film that explores various abstract themes. It has become very popular in the art and philosophy worlds.

09. We consider our pet dog a family member and not simply _____.

10. The church began construction _____ 1500 AD.

LESSON SEVEN

B. Fill in the blanks in the passage with the most appropriate words.
Passage 7:

The hikers gathered their _____ and made for the woods. They were an experienced group, _____ in specific survivalist skills, and yet they knew the adventure ahead would be a trying, _____ one. Among them was Steve, who specialized in rock-climbing, but who was subject to _____ arthritis—a dangerous ailment considering his hobby—plus Steve's girlfriend Nancy, who used to _____ Steve about his adrenaline-seeking recreational activities but who herself was now an avid practitioner. Mark, a _____ young man who studied medicine, and Mark's cousin Harriet, also accompanied Nancy and Steve.

It wasn't long before the foursome approached a harrowing _____. They knew they had to cross, but there was no bridge. Harriet was familiar with the area, however, and knew of an old _____ that stood between the cliff sides, which they could enter and use to cross. Like a _____ of politicians, they took a vote: continue walking east and hope they found a bridge, or head west for the citadel? In the end, they relied on Harriet's intel and started hiking west. It wasn't long before they came across the citadel, which was built _____ 1600. Amazingly, it was abandoned! They had no trouble entering, and within twenty minutes they had crossed the _____ and were on their way towards the mountains.

LESSON EIGHT

Target Words

1. Claimant
2. Cloister
3. Commodious
4. Comprise
5. Congenial
6. Connoisseur
7. Consensus
8. Coterie
9. Countenance
10. Coup

A. Fill in the blanks with the most appropriate words.

01. My aunt has played saxophone in a jazz band for over thirty years, so it's accurate to call her a _____ of jazz music.

02. She is terrible at lying. Every time she lies, her shifty _____ gives her away.

03. It was a major _____ to get such an important contract for the company; it approved that we could always successfully achieve something difficult.

04. Visible light _____ only a minute fraction of the electromagnetic spectrum.

05. The _____ insisted to the police that she had been robbed.

06. I love staying at my parents' house. It's much more _____ than my own meagre apartment.

07. They were such _____ neighbours that everyone in the subdivision was sad when they decided to move away

08. Our teacher let the class vote on where our next field trip would be, and the _____ was overwhelmingly in favor of the aquarium

09. Mrs. Neal likes to invite her _____ of college friends over for monthly dinner parties.

10. The _____ was coated in ice and could not be walked upon until it melted.

LESSON EIGHT

B. Fill in the blanks in the passage with the most appropriate words.
Passage 8:

The wine _____ was being charged with poisoning a guest at his vineyard, located at a large, bucolic _____ once home to monks. On the day of the trial, the judge, a strict but _____ man who held the law above all else, listened as the defending lawyer tried to justify the _____ egregious actions. While at the rustic, _____ vineyard, the poisoned guest had been among a _____ of friends and other wine-lovers, when the convict replaced the man's glass with a poisoned one. It had been a clever, wicked _____ de grâce that the victim could never have predicted nor desired.

_____ mainly of rat poison and bleach, the laced glass of wine was so disgusting the guest immediately spat it out, much to the surprise of the people nearby. The would-be assassin's _____ gave him away, however, and it wasn't long before the guests had cornered the man and called the police. The judge listened to the story with rapt attention, and once the lawyers had made their statements and witnesses were called, the judge and jury left the room to deliberate. The general _____ among the jury was unanimous: the man was guilty. The judge sentenced him to twenty years in prison.

LESSON NINE

Target Words

1. Couture
2. Cower
3. Cranny
4. Craven
5. Creditor
6. Criterion
7. Cubism
8. Curtail
9. Curvilinear
10. Damper

A. Fill in the blanks with the most appropriate words.

01. The gala was _____ when something caught fire, and all of the guests had to evacuate.

02. His melancholic demeanour always puts a _____ on our office parties.

03. We have never been fans of _____. It's too angular and structured for our tastes.

04. Her work conduct went against the company's professional _____, so she was let go.

05. He hated to be called _____, but he knew there was some truth to it. Just yesterday, he had screamed at the sight of a small garden spider!

06. When it comes to clothing, Eleanor prefers spending money on expensive, high _____.

07. The thunder and lightning made my dog _____ under my bed.

08. Albert's keys fell into the gutter, but the _____ between the iron bars was too narrow for him to reach into.

09. The _____ had sent Jerry three letters demanding overdue payment, and the final letter threatened legal repercussions if the bill was not paid.

10. The _____ rollercoaster sloped and arched in every direction.

LESSON NINE

B. Fill in the blanks in the passage with the most appropriate words.
Passage 9:

Planning for the gala had been a tedious affair, but finally the event was coming to fruition! Celebrating Picasso-esque _____ in Parisian haute _____, the gala was sure to bring in the biggest names in fashion and art. The chief planner was a woman named Maude. Maude never _____ before a challenge, and the gala had certainly been one of her biggest yet. Rather than feel _____ about all of the duties and responsibilities she had, she was determined to make it her most extravagant event yet. The Bank of Paris, a _____ renowned for its philanthropic work in the world of art and fashion, had donated a large sum of money to the event, which had been a big help. Their only _____ for such a charitable act had been a small mention in the program.

Maude _____ stress by beginning to plan for the gala six months in advance. She knew that being prepared would pay off in the long run, and in her experience, leaving too little time to plan often put a _____ on her general outlook on things. She didn't want any of her own personal negativities to seep into the gala. On the night of the gala, there was hardly a _____ piece of clothing, furniture, or décor in sight. Everything exuded the angularity of cubist art, and there wasn't a nook or _____ that hadn't been accounted for. By the end of the night, Maude was lauded for her attention to detail, and the gala was a huge success!

LESSON TEN

Target Words

1. Dauntless
2. Dearth
3. Debacle
4. Debase
5. Decree
6. Deduce
7. Defame
8. Deft
9. Demagogue
10. Demonic

A. Fill in the blanks with the most appropriate words.

01. I'm amazed by how _____ Nancy can be. She regularly goes on dangerous rock-climbing adventures.

02. The magazine had severely _____ the actress, so she sued them for libel.

03. Sherlock Holmes is known for his ability to _____ the solutions to elaborate mysteries.

04. The _____ demanded all citizens take an annual emissions test to determine the harmfulness of their cars' exhaust.

05. The _____ of evidence forced the police officers to release their suspect from custody.

06. Satan is said to be a fallen angel who became _____ after his exile from Heaven.

07. The president proved himself to be a true _____ after the election. He made so many promises just to rake in votes, and he never fulfilled any of them!

08. The magician switched the card from hand to hand, using a movement so _____ it was impossible to tell how he'd done it.

09. Our world view has become _____. We no longer have a sense of the sacred.

10. The dinner party was an absolute _____. The main course burnt, setting off the fire alarm, and then everyone's clothes got wet!

LESSON TEN

B. Fill in the blanks in the passage with the most appropriate words.
Passage 10:

The _____ of evidence was making it difficult to pinpoint a suspect for the murder. The detective, a _____, older woman known across the country for her _____ bravery and determination for uncovering the truth, was finding the case more and more challenging. The murderer himself was clearly no novice killer, and his crime had been executed so perfectly that the detective wondered whether this case would be her downfall.

She was able to _____ that the murderer was a man in his thirties, and that there were, perhaps, _____ reasons behind his crime. Various pieces of the puzzle contained satanic imagery, and though the disturbing scene of the crime had been a _____ sight, it was clear to her that she could not handle this _____ alone.

The detective enlisted the help of a private investigator (PI) who had been _____ for an old investigation on a satanic cult within a major corporation. The PI had sought a _____ against the CEO of the corporation, a seedy _____ of a man who had worked his way up the corporate ladder through flattery and cunning. It was this PI that helped the detective find the murderer, who in fact was an employee of the company that the PI had worked so hard to expose! By the end of the trial, the PI had been redeemed in the eyes of society, and the killer was caught.

LESSON ELEVEN

Target Words

1. Demur
2. Denounce
3. Desiccate
4. Dilemma
5. Disparage
6. Dispel
7. Disperse
8. Dissolution
9. Divine
10. Docile

A. Fill in the blanks with the most appropriate words.

01. The radio announcer _____ the rumour that his partner had left the show.

02. I threw a piece of bread into the water and watched the surprised fish quickly _____.

03. The _____ riverbed cracked dryly beneath the sun.

04. He had a serious _____: he could go to either his best friend's birthday celebration or his cousin's engagement party, but not both.

05. She tried to shut out the _____ thoughts that told her she would do horribly on the test no matter how much she studied.

06. The deer was _____ and friendly. It ate right out of our hands!

07. We can attribute the _____ of the firm to a major partner moving away.

08. Michael promised they were going in the right direction, but his girlfriend _____ when they passed the same bridge twice.

09. The traffic was so terrible that I'm convinced it was _____ intervention that got me to my flight on time.

10. The football player _____ his allegiance to the team and quit.

LESSON ELEVEN

B. Fill in the blanks in the passage with the most appropriate words.
Passage 11:

The celebrity's publicist knew the rumours would be difficult to _____, but he wasn't prepared for how challenging this _____ really would be. The rumours had come from an unknown source who had gone to multiple _____ tabloid magazines with the fake news of the celebrity's pregnancy. From there, the tabloids had _____ the rumours far and wide through their print magazines, online blogs, social media, and now, word-of-mouth.

At first, the publicist's client asked him to put out a statement _____ the pregnancy rumour, but when that didn't work, they realized they would have to find another way to effect the _____ of this damaging gossip. The publicist's client was a young, _____ woman who was relatively new to the realm of Hollywood, and therefore somewhat naïve to the nefarious ways of tabloid magazines. When the publicist asked if she might be willing to discuss the rumours on a daytime television talk show, she _____. She only wanted to discuss her upcoming movie, not unfounded rumours. In the end, as if by _____ intervention, a picture of her was taken by paparazzi and, in the picture, there was no sign of a baby bump. Robbed of their credibility, the devilish rumours became _____, and at last were laid to rest.

LESSON TWELVE

Target Words

1. Doldrums
2. Domain
3. Dormant
4. Draconian
5. Dromedary
6. Dulcet
7. Duress
8. Edifice
9. Efface
10. Egalitarian

A. Fill in the blanks with the most appropriate words.

01 The cat chased the mouse, who was surely under great _____.

02 The politician claimed to be a/an _____, but it was clear he played favourites.

03 His _____ is obviously the city. He is rattled by the silence and isolation of rural life.

04 She spoke in a soft, _____ tone that made me feel that everything would be ok.

05 Anger and jealousy can lie _____ in a person for years before bubbling to the surface.

06 Carrie had been stuck in the _____ ever since she failed the big exam, so her mom took her for ice cream in hopes that it would cheer her daughter up.

07 It's amazing how such vast, commanding _____ as the Great Wall of China have stood the test of time.

08 We wrote our names in the sand, but the tide came in and _____ our signatures.

09 The _____ lay in a shaded part of the farm and waited patiently for its dinner.

10 They have a _____ approach to parenting: their rules are rigid, and the punishment is severe if they are broken.

LESSON TWELVE

B. Fill in the blanks in the passage with the most appropriate words.
Passage 12:

Despite being near such a grand _____ as the Great Pyramid of Giza and riding atop a sand-coloured _____, Allen could not help but feel underwhelmed. He had been in the _____ for months and had in fact begun taking antidepressant medication as a precaution, but so far it had not helped much. He had once been a cheerful young man, able to suppress his low spirits with ease; however, those unhappy thoughts had lain _____ for so long that they inevitably came to the surface in his middle age.

Although his blues put his happiness under _____, he tried not to think about it because that would only make it worse. Instead, he relied on his partner of fifteen years, George, who was an exceptionally kind man with a _____ voice that always seemed to calm Allen. George's _____ outlook on the world helped Allen see the brighter side of things. His own bleak outlook on the world was slowly being _____ thanks to George.

As they neared the pyramids, George looked over at Allen from his own camel and smiled. The _____ heat in Egypt was making Allen feel unwell, but George's smile was like a cold drink of water and Allen couldn't help but smile back at his partner. Though they were in Egypt, far from their home and in a strange, sweltering, unknown _____, Allen felt his melancholy slip away momentarily, and he found contentment in their Egyptian adventure.

LESSON THIRTEEN

Target Words

1. Elapse
2. Elfin
3. Embellish
4. Embody
5. Emit
6. Emulate
7. Endure
8. Engulf
9. Enrage
10. Enrapture

A. Fill in the blanks with the most appropriate words.

01. She has very _____ features: her eyes are large and her ears are even a bit pointed!

02. The crowd became _____ when the referee called a foul.

03. It's impossible to tell how much time has _____ without a clock in the room.

04. The little girl _____ her favourite book heroine whenever she is worried or afraid.

05. How much must we _____ before our debts are repaid?

06. The teapot _____ a high-pitched whistle when the water has boiled.

07. Tommy is _____ by the idea of becoming a movie star.

08. I am always able to tell when Cindy _____ something. She gets an impish look in her eye.

09. Mark _____ the perfect basketball player: he's light on his feet and incredibly tall.

10. The kitchen fire got out of hand, and soon the house was _____ in flames.

LESSON THIRTEEN

B. Fill in the blanks in the passage with the most appropriate words.
Passage 13:

Ella was an especially talented ballet dancer. She had the petite _____ figure so synonymous with ballet dancers, and she was the _____ of grace. This winter, she would be dancing in the _____ Swan Lake ballet, a prestigious honour for any acclaimed dancer. As time _____ however, apprehensions about her performance _____ her. She wanted to be sure she could do every move precisely, so most nights she stayed at the ballet studio longer than any other dancers to practice. Her dedication and _____ were true testament to her appreciation for dance.

With her performance only a week away, her nervousness began to dwindle as she grew more and more confident in her ability to _____ the dance moves as best she could. One day, the costume designer for the ballet called her in for a fitting. The designer showed Ella the costumes she would be wearing for her performance. They were _____ with sequins and lace, each more magnificent than the last. Ella was in awe of the majesty each costume _____. She knew that she had to perform perfectly, if only to do those beautiful costumes justice!

And so, she spent the last week of practice working harder than ever before. She knew that if she messed up, she would be _____ with herself and bring shame to her dance company. But in the end, she performed so spectacularly that she was scouted by Broadway talent managers.

LESSON FOURTEEN

Target Words

1. Ensemble
2. Entice
3. Entomb
4. Entomology
5. Entreat
6. Erudite
7. Euphonious
8. Evade
9. Evoke
10. Exhume

A. Fill in the blanks with the most appropriate words.

01. The painting _____ strong feelings of discomfort and chaos.

02. The wife _____ her husband not to go on the perilous expedition.

03. Though he was tired and disheveled, the prospect of a free dinner at the soup kitchen was too _____ for him to pass up.

04. I don't know how some people can study _____. Bugs are creepy!

05. Perfectly _____ in a cast of fossilized tree sap, the antediluvian bird would aid scientists all across the world in their research of prehistoric animals.

06. The club is reserved for the most _____ members of society. You have to take an exam just to get an interview!

07. The creek outside her window was a _____ soundtrack that lulled her to sleep each night.

08. No matter what, the president found ways to _____ the most pressing questions.

09. Many artifacts were _____ during the excavation of Pompeii.

10. The woodwind _____ played a complicated piece of music that earned them a standing ovation.

LESSON FOURTEEN

B. Fill in the blanks in the passage with the most appropriate words.
Passage 14:

Though many of Irina's female friends detested bugs, Irina found them fascinating. Because of this, she decided to study _____ at the university level. Her mother and father were anthropologists and _____ Irina to study anthropology instead, but Irina was steadfast. There was something _____ about all of those creepy-crawlies, and besides, Irina had never been bothered by insects. At the age of ten, she was unashamedly _____ about bugs, and by the time she graduated high school, the prospect of studying anything besides insects had been, in her mind, all but laid to rest and _____.

Irina preferred to work and research alone, but during her first few years at university she found she actually enjoyed _____ research and experimentation. Many of the other students in her program were equally fascinated by bugs, and before long she had many friends! Gone were the days when she had to _____ the topic of wasps, ants, cockroaches, and bees. Her friends enjoyed discussing the same things as she, which was a _____ relief. As the years went on, she _____ from herself more and more passion for entomology. And from her friends, who _____ the same passion, she found comfort and reassurance that she could truly be herself and study what she wanted without judgment.

LESSON FIFTEEN

Target Words

1. Expunge
2. Facilitate
3. Fathom
4. Fawn
5. Feign
6. Fester
7. Fetish
8. Fickle
9. Fjord
10. Fleece

A. Fill in the blanks with the most appropriate words.

01. It's fair to say his _____ is strange foods. He's tried everything from fish eyes to cow tongue!

02. There was no way we would be able to cross the _____ before the sun went down, so we set up camp.

03. Ella _____ enthusiasm when she opened the gift her grandmother got her: a sweater that was two sizes too small and an atrocious shade of yellow.

04. The protesters knew that in order to spread their cause, they would need to _____ a more widespread protest.

05. She could not _____ how he had managed to get a driver's license when he couldn't even parallel park!

06. If you don't clean the wound, it will _____.

07. _____ is a great fabric to wear in the winter because it keeps you warm.

08. The newborn _____ still had white spots on its fur to camouflage it from predators.

09. She has _____ taste in books. One minute she loves an author, the next she's throwing away all of that author's books.

10. He desperately wished there was a way to _____ his responsibility in the matter, but in the end, he knew he would have to face the consequences.

LESSON FIFTEEN

B. Fill in the blanks in the passage with the most appropriate words.
Passage 15:

It was fair to say that camping and hiking were an obsession for both Mandy and Caroline, to the point that it could almost be considered a _____! The two women went on camping adventures every weekend, like clockwork. It was hard to _____ the number of parks and trails they had traversed. Nor were they _____; no river current was too daunting, no _____ was too wide to cross, and no mountain too tall. For them, being in nature was a way to _____ the desolate malaise that plagued their weekday work lives. Hiking and camping _____ resilience in every other aspect of their lives, so it was no wonder they did it so often!

That particular week, Mandy and Caroline decided to visit Mount Rainier National Park in Washington State. The idea to scale Mt. Rainier had been in their minds for so long, they were worried it was going to _____, so they decided to go once the summer season was over and most tourists had evacuated the park. But when they arrived at the park, it was dreadfully cold. No amount of wool or _____ clothing could prepare them for the hike up the mountain.

At first, they _____ enthusiasm for the climb, with neither one of them wanting to put a damper on the trip. But after hiking up the mountain for three hours, it was just too cold to continue! Even the animals had found warm places to stay: there wasn't a bird, a bear, or a _____ in sight! So, Mandy and Caroline called it quits and headed back to their hotel, where they spent the rest of their trip reading books by the fire and for once enjoying a quiet, relaxing weekend together.

LESSON SIXTEEN

Target Words

1. Forage
2. Forbear
3. Forsake
4. Fortuitous
5. Fraught
6. Gamin
7. Gazebo
8. Generalize
9. Giddy
10. Girdle

A. Fill in the blanks with the most appropriate words.

01. After hearing the news of an airplane crash, Michelle was _____ with worry about her flight the next day.

02. When his friends all left camp without him, Darren felt _____ and paltry.

03. Squirrels are excellent _____. They are more resourceful than people give them credit for!

04. Maddy was _____ with excitement when she won the gold medal for best science project.

05. It's not smart to make _____ about people from certain ethnic backgrounds. You might offend them, and your perceptions might be wrong.

06. Rick had made a complete turnabout. He had gone from being a wretched _____ to manager of a bookstore in less than ten months!

07. Dale and Diane loved their new house but thought the _____ in the backyard was tacky and needed to be taken down.

08. The Ring of Fire is the chain of volcanoes which _____ the Pacific.

09. I can only _____ from asking them about the gossip for so long. I'm dying to know what happened!

10. It was a _____ mistake that she bought a train ticket on the wrong day.

LESSON SIXTEEN

B. Fill in the blanks in the passage with the most appropriate words.
Passage 16:

Like an outcast _____ shunned from society, Dean had been stuck on the deserted island for over a month now. In the beginning, he had been _____ with worry about when he would be rescued, but after not seeing a single ship for weeks on end, he realized how truly _____ he was. At first, he had been _____ with nervousness about how he would survive on his own, but he thought back to his survivalist days in the Boy Scouts, which in the end would be his most valuable and _____ faculty.

The Boy Scout survivalist lessons had taught him that to _____ about the edibility of plants could be deadly. Thankfully, the island housed coconut palm trees and various berry bushes, which he _____ daily. As more time passed, he became more skilled, and eventually he even crafted a _____ out of tree boughs, leaves, and mud! At night he slept beneath a makeshift tent, having woven a _____ of vines to hold the poles together. During the days he purified seawater and hunted whatever small game he could. Then one day, after over six months on the island, a ship anchored! He had been _____ his ordeal for so long that he was in disbelief when a rescue party actually landed! The captain of the ship invited him aboard with open arms, and Dean was given a warm meal, a hot shower, and a real bed to sleep in.

LESSON SEVENTEEN

Target Words

1. Girth
2. Gloat
3. Glutton
4. Gossamer
5. Grandiloquent
6. Grandiose
7. Guile
8. Guise
9. Harangue
10. Harrowing

A. Fill in the blanks with the most appropriate words.

01. The documentary gave a _____ look into the lives of gang members in Detroit.

02. Under the _____ of a lawyer, she sneaked into the police evidence room.

03. Despite his _____ efforts to prove his love, she ultimately rejected him.

04. I would hate to be considered a _____, though I often have trouble controlling my cravings.

05. She couldn't stop _____ about her recent tennis match win.

06. The doctor measured the _____ of his patient's waist, which was enough to convince the patient to start a diet.

07. Unsurprisingly, his charm and _____ got him out of a tricky situation.

08. _____ cobwebs lined the autumn trees, which rustled in the wind.

09. The male peacock fans out its _____ array of colourful feathers in hopes it will attract a female.

10. Mark was fired because he would sometimes _____ customers who came into the store.

LESSON SEVENTEEN

B. Fill in the blanks in the passage with the most appropriate words.
Passage 17:

Jade and I went to the zoo yesterday. We had heard about how _____ it was, and the astonishing number of species housed there was too enticing to pass up. The zoo was, in fact, a rehabilitation sanctuary where hundreds of animals could roam comfortably in natural habitats and receive the best medical treatments whenever necessary.

First, we saw the birds. The peacock was the most interesting. The males have a _____ array of _____ feathers that fan out behind them as they walk. Though narcissism is often epitomized by the image of a peacock, I found they were not such pompous, _____ animals as often thought to be. As with narcissism itself, pride is a _____ that leads to misunderstanding. Its fan of iridescent feathers was a thing of beauty, and the _____ was enormous; I could only feel wonderment that such splendour could appear on a creature of the earth.

Jade's favourite animal is the tiger, though, which I find intimidating. While at the zoo, we came upon their cages at feeding time. Tigers are enormous creatures with razor-sharp fangs and a hunter's _____, but as we watched them eat, I felt nauseated by their _____. To my sensitive ears, their roars were like a _____. Jade noticed that watching the beastly carnivorous cats was too _____ for me, so we left them to inspect other less aggressive animals.

LESSON EIGHTEEN

Target Words

1. Herbicide
2. Histrionic
3. Hoard
4. Hovel
5. Husbandry
6. Idiosyncrasy
7. Impede
8. Incite
9. Incongruous
10. Infamy

A. Fill in the blanks with the most appropriate words.

01 Her scandalous role in the upcoming film granted her _____ she would be unable to escape for years.

02 Gerard was known for his conscientious _____ of all kinds of farm animals. He had a knack for caring for them.

03 The _____ had caved in after a storm and left many homeless people without shelter.

04 The venomous snake's poison can _____ a person's ability to breathe.

05 Parents declared the new video game a bad influence, claiming it would _____ violence in the schoolyard.

06 She spent hours putting together an outfit for the gala, but in the end her ensemble was an _____ mess of different fabrics.

07 One of my most habitual _____ is checking the back seat whenever I get into my car.

08 He _____ old baseball cards because he thought he might be able to sell them for twice their value one day.

09 The farmer sprayed his plants with _____ in hopes it would deter further damage to his crops.

10 The singer's _____ outpouring of emotion was too much for me to take seriously.

106

LESSON EIGHTEEN

B. Fill in the blanks in the passage with the most appropriate words.
Passage 18:

The reality TV show was about people who have a _____ problem. The host would travel to the homes of people who were unable to throw away, sell, or get rid of any possessions until their houses were full to the brim with junk and meaningless memorabilia. These _____ had become claustrophobic from the sheer number of things piled all over the place. Often, they were so messy and cluttered that they _____ a person's ability to walk through rooms. The people who lived there usually didn't see how badly their homes were in disarray, and instead either didn't acknowledge the mess or else found it merely _____. Other times the host would unintentionally _____ an aggressive response from these hoarders, who saw nothing wrong with their hygiene habits and became defensive when provoked.

One of the most _____ episodes of the reality show was when the host visited a house so appallingly disheveled that weeds were actually growing under and through the trims of the house! A team had all but doused the entire house in _____ to kill the weeds, and the usually _____ host was grim with disgust. It was as though the occupants had been practicing pest _____! By the end of almost every episode, the host would bring in a cleaning team to provide the living space with some much-needed organization, until the place once again had a clean floor space, carpet and cabinets. The show was satisfying to many viewers because of how quickly and thoroughly the host and his cleaning team could take a pigsty and scrub it to an _____ state of refinement.

LESSON NINETEEN

Target Words

1. Insouciant
2. Intervene
3. Inveigle
4. Irascible
5. Joust
6. Karma
7. Laconic
8. Lament
9. Languish
10. Lassitude

A. Fill in the blanks with the most appropriate words.

01. It was pure _____ that she got a ticket after running the red light.

02. When he said he was going to pull the prank, I tried to _____ because I knew it could go wrong.

03. The awards show had a moment of silence to _____ the loss of a beloved writer.

04. A lack of sunlight and water will cause houseplants to _____ and wither away.

05. Cindy caught the flu. _____ and a high fever were two of the side effects.

06. The voters appreciated his _____ approach to debate because it made him seem thoughtful.

07. She is known for being an _____ woman with a serious temper.

08. The magician _____ the audience member into being his assistant for the trick.

09. My _____ in this particular matter does not mean I am uncaring about everything.

10. The medieval carnival would host an exciting _____ match.

LESSON NINETEEN

B. Fill in the blanks in the passage with the most appropriate words.
Passage 19:

Dean and Sam were always _____ with one another for some reason or another. They were both _____ to begin with, and argumentative to boot! Though their altercations would begin in the same _____, taciturn ways, they always resorted to violence. It seemed like _____ then that one day their fighting actually got them locked in jail for a night. Dean and Sam had been outside of a pub fighting when a bystander tried to _____. The bystander ought to have kept _____ about Dean and Sam's quarrel, however, because Dean accidentally ended up punching the man in the stomach! The man slumped to the ground as if struck by sudden _____ and ceased moving.

Soon people gathered around Dean, Sam, and the man who lay _____ on the ground. It wasn't long before police arrived. Despite their attempts to _____ the police into letting them go, Dean and Sam were arrested for fighting in public and assault of a stranger. That night in jail, the two men apologized to each other for fighting, and _____ their thoughtless actions which had landed them in a locked cell.

LESSON TWENTY

Target Words

1. Laudable
2. Lax
3. Legacy
4. Lesion
5. Lethargy
6. Lexicon
7. Lieu
8. Loiter
9. Maim
10. Marauder

A. Fill in the blanks with the most appropriate words.

01. The rules at the camp are _____, which was enough for Mrs. Rogers to reconsider allowing her young, mischievous boy to attend that summer.

02. Doctors and nurses have an ornate _____ when it comes to medical terms.

03. In _____ of cash, I decided to pay for my meal with a credit card.

04. The _____ were always up to no good, and regularly sneaked out of bed to explore the castle.

05. The storm outside made me _____, so I stayed inside and read a book.

06. Having a star named after this scientist confirmed his _____.

07. Her poem was a _____ piece of art that eventually won a literature prize!

08. The criminal had stabbed a man and caused a fatal _____, which was egregious enough for the attacker to be sentenced to life in prison.

09. Mall security workers are serious about _____. They will not allow it.

10. The soldiers who made it out of the battle alive did not escape without serious _____.

LESSON TWENTY

B. Fill in the blanks in the passage with the most appropriate words.
Passage 20:

Remus was _____ and only wanted to sleep, but his friends woke him up from his dorm late one night to _____ around the boarding school after-hours. Begrudgingly, in _____ of sleeping that night, Remus joined his friends. As they crept around the library, the _____ group of boys evaded the watchful eyes of hall monitors and late-night studiers. Their ability to be quiet and remain unseen was almost _____, though not in the eyes of the professor who found them wandering around on a forbidden floor.

This professor, though usually somewhat _____ in the classroom, was furious to see Remus and his friends there. After admonishing them harshly with a _____ of furious remarks, he sent the boys back to their rooms for the night. Remus, shamed by the verbal _____ that had occurred, was worried all that night until the following morning. His first class of the day was with the professor who had caught them, and he was anxious to see whether he and his friends' late-night antics had left a _____ in the teacher's mind. However, the professor had since suffered a _____ to his hand, and was not in class for the next few days. By the time the professor returned to his teaching position, he had completely forgotten about Remus and his friends' mischievousness!

LESSON TWENTY-ONE

Target Words

1. Marshal
2. Martyr
3. Masticate
4. Melancholy
5. Menagerie
6. Migratory
7. Milieu
8. Mirage
9. Misanthropy
10. Misnomer

A. Fill in the blanks with the most appropriate words.

01. Despite how _____ she looks, Tara is actually a very pleasant person!

02. If you do not _____ your food, you're liable to choke!

03. Monarch butterflies are _____ insects that flock to warmer climates during the winter months.

04. He considered himself a _____ for being arrested at the protest in lieu of his cohorts.

05. The commander _____ his troops so that he could discuss their tactics.

06. The cartoon showed a man stranded in the desert and walking towards a _____ of his own imagining.

07. The politician's _____ was obvious enough to anyone who scrutinized his lack of participation in humanitarian causes.

08. Koala bears are marsupials, not bears. This common _____ continues to be used when referring to the furry animals.

09. The new antique store stocked a _____ of odds and ends, and everyone was drawn to its strange wares.

10. The debate of nature versus nurture seeks to determine how important a person's biology and _____ are when it comes to their personality.

LESSON TWENTY-ONE

B. Fill in the blanks in the passage with the most appropriate words.
Passage 21:

Cora had grown up in a rural _____ that played host to a number of wild species, so she was no stranger to the _____ residing at the wildlife rescue centre. There were many species of _____ birds such as swans, geese, and ducks of every kind, and mammals _____ in separate, roomy habitats that perfectly suited each animal's specific needs. Cora loved the animal sanctuary. She loved to watch the koalas _____ boughs of bamboo, see the sea lions dive into the water, and gaze at the elephants as they splashed muddy water on themselves with their long trunks. The founder, a warm-hearted, benevolent _____ of a woman named Sue, had been working with all of the animals for decades when she decided to create the sanctuary.

Cora herself had become something of a _____ since volunteering there. She hated to see injured animals come into the sanctuary when, more often than not, the injuries were caused by careless humans, whether hunters or poachers. These mishaps made her _____, but Sue told Cora that calling all humans negligent and apathetic was a generalization and a _____. Sue reasoned that many people really did care about animals because she had an overabundance of volunteers at the sanctuary! The notion that all humans were indifferent to the wellbeing of animals was just a _____ brought on by indignation and shortsightedness.

LESSON TWENTY-TWO

Target Words

1. Mode
2. Mores
3. Muse
4. Muster
5. Myriad
6. Nepotism
7. Noisome
8. Noxious
9. Oblique
10. Obtuse

A. Fill in the blanks with the most appropriate words.

01. The bookstore contained a _____ of novels, and Stacy found it hard to choose because of the wide array.

02. It was a/an _____ assumption that made the boy look stupid.

03. The car emitted so much _____ gas that it failed the emissions test.

04. Our _____ neighbours refuse to clean up after their dogs when their dogs use our front yard as a bathroom.

05. Don passed the company onto his son, which is a clear case of _____.

06. My preferred _____ of transportation is train, but there are few trains in America, so I mostly travel by air or by car.

07. The artist cited his ex-lover as a _____ for his new art installation.

08. Cody could not _____ up enough courage to go into the haunted house.

09. The small town had strange _____ that tourists couldn't get accustomed to.

10. The bodybuilder never forgets to exercise his _____ abdominal muscles.

LESSON TWENTY-TWO

B. Fill in the blanks in the passage with the most appropriate words.
Passage 22:

Jacob had been working at the company for a year when he started to catch on to some of the unsavoury _____ of the job. It was clear that the CEO firmly believed in _____, for he promoted his son at every chance until finally his son became CFO of the company. The CEO claimed his son was his _____ and his successor, and Jacob grew annoyed when the son began implementing new rules. One of the more _____ new rules had been a change in dress code, which dictated that all women must wear heels and all men three-piece suits. When employees expressed dissatisfaction, they were either suspended or fired. This _____ practice of firing employees without hearing their complaints became so commonplace that a _____ of people had simply quit their jobs.

Jacob began to wonder if an _____ approach to the new rules might have a better end result. He _____ up some gall and wrote an anonymous letter to the CEO, who was the father and patriarch of the company. He figured an anonymous _____ of communication would yield better results, and he was right! The CEO abolished all the _____ new rules his son had enacted and sent out a public apology to his employees, guaranteeing that any person fired could come back without penalty!

LESSON TWENTY-THREE

Target Words

1. Opportune
2. Optimum
3. Orthodox
4. Ostracize
5. Oust
6. Paradox
7. Paranoia
8. Parry
9. Partition
10. Penitent

A. Fill in the blanks with the most appropriate words.

01. Her love of the beach and fear of swimming were an unfortunate _____.

02. Tyson's _____ had reached dangerous levels, so he sought help from a therapist.

03. I had a six-hour layover in Chicago, which gave me _____ time to go see a movie, get lunch, and then return to the airport.

04. The boarding school has very _____ rules when it comes to co-ed living spaces.

05. Meg thought she could _____ the competition by sabotaging them, but it only got her disqualified.

06. Christmas is the _____ time to see family, though the highways and airports are usually packed with other families doing the same thing!

07. After tattling on her friends for breaking the rules, Carrie was _____ by all of them for being a blabbermouth.

08. In the Bible, it is said that only the pure and _____ will gain entry to Heaven.

09. Jordan was an excellent swordsman who could _____ an attack with borderline supernatural agility.

10. Back in the 1980s, the German Democratic Republic _____ the country into eastern and western halves.

LESSON TWENTY-THREE

B. Fill in the blanks in the passage with the most appropriate words.
Passage 23:

The Republic of Aldovia has been _____ between southern and northern countries for decades. Despite their proximity, however, both governments remain wary and _____ of the other's intentions. North Aldovia, itself a strange place led by an authoritarian president, has been _____ by most countries for its _____ and even cruel treatment of its citizens. Every year citizens try to flee North Aldovia, but their attempts to extricate themselves are usually futile, and often end in violence. It is not known whether there has ever been an attempt to _____ the president himself. That people should seek to flee from one country to another when they were once the same nation forms a tragic _____ of the Aldovian identity.

There have, however, been a few attempts to expose the inhuman treatment of North Aldovia's citizens. Reporters have tried to gain entry, but only a small handful have been granted the _____ amount of access and insight into life inside those strict borders. Many citizens are reticent and _____ overly intrusive questions about their country or the president, but there have been triumphant attempts to pry out confidential details about the goings-on in North Aldovia. In a documentary by Victory magazine, a few _____ citizens expressed subtle despondency about their life in North Aldovia. Meanwhile, it seems as though South Aldovia hopes to find some _____ plan of action to liberate and house refugees who have escaped the clutches of their alienated sister land.

LESSON TWENTY-FOUR

Target Words

1. Periphery
2. Permeate
3. Perverse
4. Petulant
5. Philanthropy
6. Phobia
7. Photogenic
8. Pied
9. Pillage
10. Pique

A. Fill in the blanks with the most appropriate words.

01 For some people, _____ is not merely a charitable hobby, but a way of life.

02 His _____ of clowns prevents him from going to the carnival.

03 Out of my _____ vision, I thought I saw the shadow behind me move.

04 The preview for the movie _____ Ben and Jerry's interest so much that they decided to go see it that very day.

05 She named her _____ dog Spots because of his dual colouration.

06 Models must be _____ because they are constantly having their picture taken.

07 He had a _____ desire to pull the fire alarm, despite knowing the consequences of doing so in the absence of a fire.

08 Social media has _____ so many parts of our lives that we can hardly discern its effects anymore.

09 The pirates _____ the town and stole everything of value.

10 The mother was sick of her child's ongoing _____, so she got a babysitter and spent the day relaxing by herself at the spa.

LESSON TWENTY-FOUR

B. Fill in the blanks in the passage with the most appropriate words.
Passage 24:

Despite my attempts to dissuade my roommate Kelly from seeing the new horror movie, I was dragged to the theatre that night around 8PM. Earlier that day we had been watching an annual fashion show full of _____ supermodels when suddenly a commercial for the movie came on the television. It had so _____ her interest that she bought tickets for us both right then and there. She thought buying a movie ticket for me was some twisted act of _____, despite the fact that I absolutely did not want to see it. The movie was about giant mutant spiders, and I had a huge _____ of all arachnids. In my opinion, spiders are _____, creepy little insects, but Kelly didn't care.

After seeing the movie, I kept checking my _____ for spiders, and weeks later I'm still mad at Kelly for making me see it. My fear of spiders used to _____ all aspects of my life until I went to therapy, but now my _____ has returned in full. I am _____ and skittish all the time; my favorite _____, polka-dot bedspread now resembles spiders in my fearful mind; and even my dreams are _____ by visions of tarantulas, black widows, and brown recluses. I think I will make Kelly pay for my next round of therapy!

LESSON TWENTY-FIVE

Target Words

1. Plight
2. Porcine
3. Potentate
4. Precarious
5. Procrastinate
6. Proficient
7. Propulsive
8. Prowess
9. Quandary
10. Queue

A. Fill in the blanks with the most appropriate words.

01 Her musical _____ was a sight to behold and a treasure to hear.

02 You will only become _____ in a language if you practice and study.

03 The car was balanced _____ on the edge of the cliff, and anything so much as a sigh was likely to push it over the edge.

04 Commemorating the _____ of Indigenous peoples is an important way of lamenting their hardships.

05 In the days of old, English _____ were powerful leaders whose decrees could quite literally change the world.

06 The once-thin Tomas has gained sixty pounds in the past year. He now looks somewhat _____.

07 British people are thought to be polite and patient, so it's no wonder they form such organized _____!

08 You'll be a lot less stressed out if you quit _____ about your homework and get it done now.

09 The cruise ship has an impressive _____ engine, so it always arrives at its destination on time.

10 She was in a bit of a _____: she could either sell her car, or she could keep it and fix everything that was broken.

LESSON TWENTY-FIVE

B. Fill in the blanks in the passage with the most appropriate words.
Passage 25:

My mom and sister were determined to find the best sales on Black Friday, though I couldn't really care less. Regardless, I joined them on their shopping excursion, knowing it would be a stressful _____. They were such _____ shoppers, however, that they could have been considered professionals! They were practically _____ of boutiques, malls, and department stores when it came to their _____ in finding great deals, and they got in and out of shops with such _____ speed and seasoned expertise that I thought it would make the _____ Black Friday endeavour a little less intimidating for someone like me. Besides, I had _____ about my Christmas shopping in earlier years, so I decided it would be a good idea to get a head start on all of it this time.

The first place we went to was an outlet-clothing store known to carry high-end brands for great prices. When we arrived, however, there was a long _____ that stretched nearly the length of the store! Though I considered the long line a _____, my mom and sister weren't as perturbed; we were armed with coffee and patience. As we strolled through the store, my sister picked up various pieces of clothing. She was shopping for her husband, an athletic young man. She showed me and my mom an oversized pinkish sweater that she wanted to buy for him, but we told her it might make him look _____. She decided we were right, and laughed it off.

LESSON TWENTY-SIX

Target Words

1. Quirk
2. Quixotic
3. Ramification
4. Relinquish
5. Reminisce
6. Remorse
7. Resurgent
8. Revere
9. Rivet
10. Roster

A. Fill in the blanks with the most appropriate words.

01. On their fifth-year anniversary, Eric and Laura _____ about their wedding day and how wonderful it had been.

02. There are serious _____ when it comes to plagiarism, so don't even think about it!

03. The film was a _____ horror movie whose protagonist was a deaf woman fighting for her life against a nefarious masked assailant.

04. The teacher ticked students' names off a _____ for the daily roll call.

05. Lately there has been a _____ of fashion from the 1990s.

06. One of his wife's more annoying _____ was to clip her nails on the living room sofa.

07. The reality TV star was reluctant to _____ her fame, so she debased herself in public settings in order to retain the media's attention.

08. The University of Oxford is a highly _____ institution that has many notable alumni who have gone on to become Prime Ministers or Nobel laureates.

09. Karen had _____ dreams about her ideal wedding, all of which would be nearly impossible to finance.

10. The driver showed no _____ for hitting his neighbour's mailbox with his car, which only served to infuriate the neighbour.

LESSON TWENTY-SIX

B. Fill in the blanks in the passage with the most appropriate words.
Passage 26:

Billy had been suspended from school, but his _____ into the public school system was fast approaching, and his mother was worried. Billy had already been expelled from two different high schools and most recently had been suspended from a third for bullying students. Billy rarely ever showed _____ for his actions, and even more rarely did he consider the _____. When Billy had first begun showing signs of anger issues, his mother thought she could enroll Billy in sports and _____ those problems to his coaches. This had only increased Billy's aggressiveness, however, which was an unfortunate _____ she had not anticipated.

She frequently _____ about the days before Billy had shown signs of hostility, and had _____ dreams that he would one day wake up and suddenly be the sweet, compassionate young boy he had been in his youth. As Billy's reappearance at school neared, his mother was _____ with anxiety about how things would go and whether he would be expelled a third time. But something strange happened: Billy met a girl named Claire. Claire went to a _____ private high school downtown. She was an ambitious young woman whose _____ of dreams was lengthy, impressive, and apparently inspiring for Billy. It wasn't long before Claire and Billy began dating, and by the time Billy started school again, he had come to resemble a semblance of the empathetic young man his mother had once known him to be.

LESSON TWENTY-SEVEN

Target Words

1. Rudimentary
2. Scapegoat
3. Scrutinize
4. Segregate
5. Serpentine
6. Sombre (US Somber)
7. Sonorous
8. Spur
9. Spurn
10. Stupefy

A. Fill in the blanks with the most appropriate words.

01 The politician tried to use his campaign team as a _____, but it was clear the mistake was his own doing.

02 The elevator's _____ music lulled the baby to sleep.

03 Funerals are always _____ affairs, and it's even worse if it's raining.

04 Their first chemistry class covered the most _____ concepts so that everyone would understand the take-home assignment.

05 The wealthy actor was _____ after he gave his fiancée a tiny engagement ring.

06 The singer left the audience _____ when she sang the most difficult part of the entire opus perfectly.

07 Cowboys traditionally wore _____ on their boots, which they used to direct their horses.

08 The rollercoaster was a _____ nightmare with so many ups and downs that all it took was one look before Jeremy decided he would never go on it.

09 Despite the fact that she had _____ his advances a dozen times, Cole kept asking her out on dates.

10 _____ schools in the southern states of America were said to be "separate but equal," but many people knew that it still constituted racism.

LESSON TWENTY-SEVEN

B. Fill in the blanks in the passage with the most appropriate words.
Passage 27:

Edie had never gone snowboarding before but was desperate to try it out, so she signed up for private lessons. The lessons were taught by a laid-back guy in his late 20s with a _____, commanding voice perfect for teaching out on the snowy, hushed slopes. During the first lesson, her instructor taught her the most _____ aspects of snowboarding, such as how to clip your shoes onto the board, and how to stand up once you were strapped in. Edie _____ each instruction with _____ seriousness.

Once she had learned the simple act of strapping in and standing up, her instructor proceeded to teach her how to stop and start on the board when going down hills. He then showed Edie how to do _____ turns that amazed and _____ her so much that she began to feel intimidated. Her instructor told Edie to relax, and that falling was natural for novice snowboarders. Edie hoped to use the slick patches of ice as a _____ for her multiple spills and tumbles, but eventually she accepted the fact that it was ok if she fell dozens of times—she was a beginner!

The slope was _____ between beginners and intermediate snowboarders, and eventually Edie's instructor had them move onto the intermediate side of the slope. Edie _____ this decision at first, but her instructor reassured her. He told her that she was ready, and promised a mug of hot chocolate as a _____ if she could make it down the hill all by herself. Edie took a deep breath and gave it her best shot. She fell two or three times, but in the end, she made it all the way down the hill!

LESSON TWENTY-EIGHT

Target Words

1. Sundry
2. Supplant
3. Surfeit
4. Tether
5. Torque
6. Trenchant
7. Truculent
8. Truncate
9. Tyro
10. Ubiquitous

A. Fill in the blanks with the most appropriate words.

01. The director has had a _____ influence on film. Many aspiring filmmakers mimic his style.

02. Laura and Chloe's wedding was a beautiful affair with lovely bouquets of flowers and a _____ of southern comfort food.

03. The dog, _____ to the pine tree, barked incessantly at the incoming storm until his owners finally let him inside.

04. She kept a _____ supply of herbs by the kitchen window, and used them in many of her recipes.

05. The lumberjack rested his axe on a _____ stump of a tree and left the forest to take a break.

06. Next door to Elena lived two young women whose _____ laughter annoyed Elena to her very core.

07. The corrupt cop manufactured evidence and used it to _____ the evidence that might have freed the man he had jailed.

08. Though John was a _____ when it came to cooking French cuisine, his crème brûlée turned out great!

09. The screw was stuck in the leg of the table, so he _____ it with as much force as he could using a screwdriver until the screw popped out.

10. Mary hated to go against Ethan in her debate class because he was unnecessarily _____.

LESSON TWENTY-EIGHT

B. Fill in the blanks in the passage with the most appropriate words.
Passage 28:

The sailor had been on _____ boats of all shapes and sizes. He had weathered _____ seas and a _____ of sunshine to the point that his skin was tan, his hands calloused, and his hair bleached blonde. He had been sailing for over twenty years, but each new adventure _____ the previous in its ability to excite and delight him. But this upcoming trip would be like one never before: he was bringing along his younger brother, a complete _____ to the ways of the sea.

The sailor assumed his younger brother wouldn't enjoy sailing across the wide, open ocean as much as he, and expected him to _____ their trip at the first sign of peril. Skills _____ in the sailing world were totally unknown to his brother, but the sailor had always gone on trips alone, so working independently would be no different than any other trip.

To his surprise, however, his brother was adamant about helping out. He was a _____ young man and was determined to do whatever necessary to ease his older sailor brother's mind and muscles for this trip. Whenever a sail or an anchor needed _____, the sailor taught his younger brother how to tie the correct knots. When the steering wheel needed extra _____ to put them in the right direction, his brother was there to lend a hand. The sailor was so impressed with his brother that he asked him to come along on his next trip across the Atlantic Ocean!

LESSON TWENTY-NINE

Target Words

1. Umbrage
2. Unbridled
3. Veer
4. Verbatim
5. Vertigo
6. Volition
7. Wane
8. Wither
9. Wrest
10. Wrath

A. Fill in the blanks with the most appropriate words.

01. Looking over the edge of tall buildings instantly gives me _____.

02. If you _____ too far off the path, you're probably going to get lost!

03. Katherine _____ the necklace from Stephanie's grip and then quickly ran away with it.

04. She neglected to water her plants for a week, so they _____ away.

05. In a moment of _____ rage, Wally thrust his fist into the wall and made a giant hole.

06. Her _____ is like the ocean during a storm; if you incur it, her rage will wash over you like a tidal wave.

07. Moe's depression finally began to _____ when he started exercising again.

08. Though he did not mean offense, Greta still took _____ at his comment.

09. My new parrot is so cool. He will repeat back whatever I say to him _____!

10. If I'm going to date him, it will be of my own _____ and not because anyone pressured me to!

LESSON TWENTY-NINE

B. Fill in the blanks in the passage with the most appropriate words.
Passage 29:

Rick wasn't the best driver, and his wife Eleanor was beginning to worry. They were driving on a winding road high up in the mountains when her _____ started to set in. As they _____ around sharp corners, she felt her courage _____ and her anxiety grow. She had no one to blame but herself; she had asked Rick to take this road, and of her own _____, because it would get them to the hotel sooner. Little did she know how _____ and riddled with pot-holes the roads would actually be.

Soon Rick detected his wife's nervousness and tried to calm her down by reciting her favorite poem _____. Eleanor loved poetry, but her apprehension and dizziness was making her nauseous. Her nausea came across as _____, so Rick stopped reciting the poem, and they rode in silence. But his silence and the bumpy roads only made her angry about their treacherous predicament, and Rick felt himself the object of her _____. Soon her anger and fear became _____ as she broke down in tears and told her husband how afraid she was of heights. Rick had never known this about his wife! He quickly pulled over to a rest area and comforted her. He practically had to _____ her from the car, but once she was out in the fresh air and took a few deep breaths, she felt her bravery set back in, and they headed back to the car.

LESSON THIRTY

Target Words

1. Wanton
2. Wily
3. Winsome
4. Wistful
5. Wizened
6. Yoke
7. Yore
8. Zealous
9. Zenith
10. Zephyr

A. Fill in the blanks with the most appropriate words.

01. The sailor looked back at the harbour with a _____ expression, unsure of when he would see land next.

02. The farmer loosened the _____ around the horses' necks and put them back into the barn for the night so they could eat and rest up.

03. The dean's speech to the graduating class was a _____ verbal attack aimed at the prime minister.

04. She was a _____ young woman with long, curly hair and bright green eyes. No man could resist her charms.

05. Joey was so _____ about the upcoming book release that he camped outside the bookstore until they opened the following morning.

06. It had been a scorching hot day, and everyone was appreciative of the _____ that billowed through the town.

07. The cartoon coyote was a _____ character who always thought he was ten steps ahead of his prey.

08. The Romans of _____ build a powerful empire that eventually saw to its own undoing.

09. Under the new ruler, the country reached its full potential. However, this _____ didn't last long, as a superior leader thereafter succeeded him.

10. Though _____ and lethargic in his old age, my grandfather was once a spry young fellow who fought valiantly in the Second World War.

LESSON THIRTY

B. Fill in the blanks in the passage with the most appropriate words.
Passage 30:

The restaurant in the hotel lobby of the recently married Tina and Marty was an upscale eatery that had received much praise and _____ reviews praising its fanciful dishes. Eating there had been the _____ of their honeymoon trip. The restaurant had an ancient Rome theme, and the décor was made to resemble the days of _____ when the Roman empire had been at its peak. The servers all wore _____ togas with ornate leather _____ across their chests. Even the cutlery was anachronistic! All of it was selected to emphasize the _____ might of the ancient Roman civilization.

After dinner, Tina and Marty sat on the beach and let a _____ of cool air wash over them. They watched a _____ couple in their early 60s stroll by the shore, and Tina smiled, hoping that would be her and Marty one day. Marty squeezed her hand and they stayed on the beach until a _____ sunset stretched out across the horizon. They stared _____ at the changing colors of the sun dancing upon the churning seas, and when it was too cold to stay out there, they went back to their hotel.

131